MASTERING MORTUARY REMOVALS

Guide – Workbook

MARCO THOMAS

Eden Logistics Inc Office: (901) 713-2650
www.EdenLogistics.biz
edenlogisticsinc@gmail.com
Editor: Melissa Nichols

DEDICATION

To the funeral industry at large, including my mentors, clients, and industry affiliates, as well as those who have trained, instructed, and shared invaluable wisdom and knowledge with me, I am deeply grateful.

To my parents, who instilled the importance of education, endurance, and consistency. Their guidance led me to understand that my potential is God-given and there are no limitations. They also instilled the value of persistence and determination despite the odds. I am truly thankful for such a dynamic cadre of supporters.

To my family and friends, I express my gratitude and love for your unwavering support.

To Funeral Service Education Students, Funeral Directors, Embalmers, and Death Care Professionals, along with countless others who tirelessly provide comfort, peace, and solace to the families we serve worldwide, I extend my heartfelt thanks.

To the Lord Jesus, I am grateful for the blessing of life and the opportunity to give back and positively impact the world.

INTRODUCTION

MASTERING MORTUARY REMOVALS

A **Removal** is the transfer of the decedent from the place of death to the funeral home or institution, facilitated and conducted by a licensed funeral director, a licensed removal company, or the county forensics office.

The funeral industry, also known as the death care industry, has an extensive history that dates back thousands of years to ancient civilizations. From ancient times to the Medieval and Renaissance periods, to the Industrial Revolution, and into the Modern Era, the practice of commemorating the life of a deceased loved one has remained a common practice. The rituals and customs surrounding death and burial have evolved significantly over time, influenced by cultural, religious, and social factors. Overall, the history of the funeral industry reflects the changing attitudes towards death and mourning throughout human history, with practices evolving to meet the needs and beliefs of each era.

Mastering Mortuary Removals was inspired by the need for timely, professional, ethical, and efficient removal services within the death care industry. As the removal and transport business sector grows to accommodate new owner-operators, this guide serves as a resource to ensure that removal service professionals maintain the highest level of professionalism and sensitivity when conducting removals in private and public spaces. The removal guide also serves as a reinforcement tool for experienced funeral directors and anyone involved in removing and transporting deceased individuals. Despite its critical role, removal service often does not receive the attention it deserves, yet it is by far the most important link in the entire process.

Removal service is about making a good first impression. It gives the removal technician the opportunity to represent the agency or funeral firm in a way that best reflects their company code of ethics. Professional removal service is so vitally important that it can have a positive or negative impact on the family of the deceased as well as the agency or firm conducting removal services. Hence, this guide aims to provide comprehensive guidance and resources for conducting removals with professionalism, ethics, and efficiency.

This guide provides comprehensive and practical scenarios that will help build confidence and increase efficiency in various removal settings, including residential and institutional removals. The guide also includes a workbook section designed to stimulate critical thinking skills, enhance problem-solving abilities, and foster professional growth within the death care industry.

CONTENTS

SECTION 2: INSTITUTIONAL REMOVALS | SCENARIOS

SAMPLES | RESIDENTIAL AND INSTITUTIONAL REMOVAL SCENARIOS

Your Favorite Undertaker

RESIDENTIAL REMOVALS

A residential removal is primarily conducted and performed at the residence, typically occurring when someone passes away at home. These removals are common among elderly individuals who pass away from natural causes, hospice care patients, or individuals who are handicapped or bedridden and require home health care. While residential removals are not as numerous as institutional and forensic removal cases, their volume varies depending on the circumstances. Deaths without suspicious activity generally result in fewer residential removals, while deaths involving violent crimes may require more removals. When a death occurs at home, there is usually an underlying health implication unless city law enforcement and medical examiner agents determine foul play or suspicion.

A residential removal can significantly impact a funeral home or medical institution, with its effects ranging from positive to negative. Conducting a removal at a residence requires the highest level of sensitivity, especially since family members are likely to be present. Sensitivity extends to various aspects, including the tone of the removal technician's voice, how condolences are expressed to the family, and the overall demeanor during the removal process. Professionalism and sensitivity are crucial, as is the practice of awareness and caution. Vigilance is essential in all residential removals due to the potential for unexpected threats. For example, a family member may be emotionally overwhelmed by the loss and could be triggered by your presence or even the sight of the cot. Additionally, a family member might become upset with the measures used to perform the removal, especially if they have chosen to witness the process. Assessing the presence of tension among family members or the influence of alcohol or drugs is also important, as these factors can interrupt the removal process. Being aware of these dynamics can help you and your assistant navigate the removal process safely and effectively, minimizing the risk of emotional outbursts.

Residential removals are diverse and can vary significantly from one another. Some removals are straightforward, while others present unique challenges that require critical thinking and problem-solving skills. The characteristics of each residence, such as space constraints, narrow halls, small rooms, or clutter, can influence the removal process. It is advisable to have two people perform residential removals to ensure the safety of the deceased and provide comfort to the family. Two-person teams reassure the family that their loved one will be handled with care and allow the family time to grieve without the burden of assisting with the removal. However, it's important to respect the family's wishes if they express a desire to participate in the removal process. Allowing family involvement can provide closure, dignity, and assurance that their loved one was respectfully and properly removed from the residence. In addition, while body bags are effective in reducing exposure and contamination risks, it's crucial to be sensitive to the family's needs and use them only when absolutely necessary. While we understand the importance from a protective and safety standpoint, it's important to recognize the potentially traumatic impact on the family. Using body bags can be emotionally sensitive and may lead to adverse emotional reactions or outbursts.

Recommended Equipment and Supplies

To enhance efficiency and effectiveness during the removal process, the following items are recommended. These supplies help mitigate risks and ensure a proper, professional removal. They should be packed and concealed in a dedicated "removal bag" or duffle bag and brought into the residence after assessing the removal setting.

Equipment
1. Mortuary Cot
2. Zip Up Cot Pouch/Cot Cover
3. Spin board *(Optional)*
4. Scissor Scoop (Optional)
5. Slider Board

Supplies
1. White linen sheets (2-3)
2. Vinyl body bags (1) Disaster Pouch (1)
3. Patient transfer sheet
4. Deodorizer (Pro Lysol spray)
5. Latex or Nitrile Gloves
6. Disposable protective coverall
7. Non-slip disposable shoe covers

8. Face mask/Face shield
9. Identification (Toe tag/Ankle band)
10. Head block and Pillow
11. Sanitizing wipes/Towels
12. Zip-Style Biohazard/Trash bag
13. Flashlight
14. Waterproof Rubber Boots

NOTE: The list of items may seem extensive, but they are crucial and necessary for a reason. When performing residential removals, you never know what challenges you may encounter. It is better to be over-prepared and equipped than to arrive at a residential removal unprepared. Often, the information provided initially is vague, lacking specific details. For instance, the first call information may include the decedent's location, weight, and positioning, but upon arrival, you may discover that the residence is highly infectious and unsanitary, and the decedent's mattress is infested with bedbugs. Therefore, it is imperative to have all the necessary equipment and supplies to carry out the removal safely and effectively.

INSTITUTIONAL REMOVALS

An institutional removal is best described as one conducted at a medical institution, which includes hospitals, nursing homes, hospice care facilities, organ/tissue procurement laboratories, and the city medical examiner/coroner's office. These removals are typically straightforward because the decedent is usually in an isolated room, such as a morgue or patient room. Additionally, you are often accompanied by nurses, physicians, and other staff members who are available to assist if needed. However, professionalism and discretion are essential, especially when the deceased is in a busy area like the emergency room, to avoid making others uncomfortable or causing fear.

When performing a removal at an institution, the decedent is usually enclosed in a body bag or covered with a sheet, simplifying the removal process. Institutions may have policies requiring the cleaning and concealment of the deceased in body bags to maintain health standards, particularly in light of diseases like COVID-19. Institutional removals typically require only one removal technician, though additional assistance may be available if needed.

In some cases, family members may remain at the institution to meet the removal technician before the removal. This can help expedite tasks such as obtaining authorization for embalming, transferring jewelry and valuables, determining the disposition of choice, and assuring the family of the professional care their loved one will receive. Institutional removals have many benefits, including the ability to gather necessary information and mitigate strenuous tasks.

The procedure for removing a decedent from an institution is usually straightforward. There is often a designated parking spot for mortuary professionals and a security escort or medical professional to guide you to and from the removal location. Documentation is typically completed upon release of the decedent into your custody, including signing a facility release form with a patient face sheet attached for your records. These face sheets are placed into the decedent's file for record-keeping and death certificate filing purposes. The primary goal during institutional removals is to maintain ethical and professional conduct.

Recommended Equipment and Supplies

The following items are recommended to enhance efficiency and effectiveness during the removal process. They help mitigate risks and ensure a proper, professional removal.

Equipment
1. Mortuary Cot
2. Zip Up Cot Pouch/Cot Cover
3. Spin board (Optional)
4. Slider Board

Supplies
1. Latex or Nitrile Gloves
2. Face mask/Face shield
3. Identification (Toe tag/Ankle band)
4. Head block and Pillow
5. Disposable protective coverall
6. White linen sheets (1-2)

NOTE: Institutional removals don't require as much preparation as residential removals because most institutions already have a supply of PPE, such as gloves, protective gowns, face masks, and body bags. However, it's still important to be well-prepared. There are instances when medical providers and institutions may run low on supplies and need to prioritize providing their staff members, such as nurses, physicians, and pathologists, with the necessary supplies first. Understanding this can help prevent delays or mishaps when conducting a removal from an institution.

Employing a system in this line of work ensures the highest level of efficiency, consistency, and, most importantly, sensitivity. Everything needs to be thought out and calculated if you should comfort families and establish a reputable and positive reputation.

8-Step Systematic Methodology

1. Assess the Situation

- Identify the location of the decedent.
- Note any environmental factors (e.g., temperature, lighting, space constraints).
- Determine the condition of the decedent (e.g., clothing, position, signs of decomposition).

2. Evaluate Safety Precautions

- Ensure personal protective equipment (PPE) is worn.
- Assess the need for additional assistance or specialized equipment (e.g., lifting devices, body bags).

3. Plan the Approach

- Determine the best approach for moving the decedent based on the scenario.
- Consider the need for coordination with other professionals or authorities or family members (e.g., medical examiner, law enforcement).

4. Identification

- Apply the correct identification to the decedent's person.

5. Execute the Removal

- Follow established protocols for handling and moving the decedent.
- Use proper lifting techniques and equipment to avoid injury.
- Maintain dignity and respect for the deceased throughout the process.

6. Document and Communicate

- Record relevant details of the removal process (e.g., condition of the decedent, any observations).
- Communicate with relevant parties (e.g., family members, funeral director, medical professional, or medical examiner) as necessary.

7. Review and Reflect

- Evaluate the removal process for areas of improvement.
- Consider any challenges faced and how they were addressed.
- Reflect on the overall experience to enhance future removals.

8. Follow-Up

- Ensure the decedent is properly transported to the designated facility.
- Complete any required documentation or paperwork associated with the removal.
- Provide any necessary support or information to the family or other involved parties.

The 8-step systematic methodology presented in this guide has been a cornerstone of my career as a mortuary transporter. When followed diligently, it guarantees the best possible outcome for both residential and institutional removals. The process is easily adaptable for institutional removals with minimal adjustment to the sequence of steps. Please refer to and review the chart in section two (2) before engaging in the institutional removal scenario exercises.

SAMPLE | RESIDENTIAL SCENARIO #1

❖ **Location:** Residence in the basement

❖ **Decedent's Weight:** 170 lbs.

❖ **Placement:** The decedent is in the bedroom in the basement area, sitting on the floor in an upright position, with their back leaned against the bed. The bedroom is extremely tight, with a king-size bed.

❖ **Duration:** The decedent has been in this position for four (4) hours

❖ **Clothing/Accessories:** The decedent is unclothed, covered with a white linen sheet

❖ **Paramedic Attendance:** The decedent was not tended to by paramedics

❖ **Gender:** Female

❖ **Special Notes:** Several family members are standing in the area, and it is very crowded and compact.

   ◇ There is a sufficient amount of space entering into the bedroom

   ◇ Police officers are present

---

1. Assess the Situation

⌑ The residence entrance door (does it prop itself?)

⌑ There is a staircase leading down into the basement

⌑ Does the bedroom door lock?

⌑ The room is extremely tight

⌑ Decedent on the floor in an upright position

⌑ No clothes on the deceased

⌑ No paramedic attendance

⌑ Signs of rigor mortis in the limbs (arms and legs)

⌑ No mouth or nose leakage or other body fluids

2. Evaluate Safety Precautions

⌑ Apply PPE, e.g., (Gloves, Facemask, and if necessary, apply a disposable coverall) Use one (1) linen sheet to wrap the decedent

3. Plan the Approach

- Considering the staircase, we will have to leave the mortuary cot on the main floor and carry the decedent to the cot
- Prepare the mortuary stretcher before conducting the removal (unfasten the straps, drape in a linen disposable sheet, place body cover to the side, and lower the cot to the waste)
- Determine who will lift the trunk and the lower extremities
- Remove the decedent from the bedroom, carry her upstairs from the basement, and lay her on the mortuary cot positioned 12 feet from the top step
- Only use assistant, no family
- Determine whether or not the family should exit the home or stay in a designated room until the removal is completed

4. Identification

- Before applying the identification, verify the correct spelling of the name with the Next of Kin (NOK) in charge
- Apply the identification bearing the specified information

5. Execute the Removal

- If determined that the removal should be private with limited visibility, kindly instruct all family members to assemble on the main floor before proceeding with the removal. Explain that they will be able to view their loved one once she is prepared and positioned on the cot if they so desire
- Make sure to close the room's door to reduce visibility and interference
- Tech One: Position your hands under the decedent's armpits from their back. Tech Two: Apply leverage to both legs towards the ankles
- Tech One: Gently push the decedent forward and lift while Tech Two pulls the decedent by the ankles. Carefully lay the decedent on their back on the floor
- The rolltuck, rollpull method should be applied. Technicians should be positioned on each side of the decedent, with the decedent lying in the middle. One technician should roll the deceased towards them while the other technician tucks a clean linen sheet (supplies) under the decedent. Afterward, the technicians should remain in position but switch roles. One technician should now roll the decedent towards them while the other technician pulls the sheet, leaving an even amount of sheet on both sides of the deceased. This should leave two corners in each technician's hand
- Each technician should tie a knot at the head and ankles of the deceased. This should position the decedent in a tacolike fashion, wrapped in the sheet, with no parts of the body exposed. Next, open the door to prepare to exit. Ensure that the space is congestion free
- Before execution, one technician should doublecheck the cot to ensure that the legs are locked so as to avoid a collapse when the decedent is placed on it
- Both technicians: Bend the knees and put arms under the decedent's body, with one person carrying the trunk and the other carrying the legs. Ensure the weight is manageable before exiting the room. Lift the decedent and exit the room, proceeding upstairs towards the cot. Gently place and position the decedent on the cot, ensuring that no skin is exposed. Fasten each buckle and tighten with care. Finally, with one technician positioned at each end of the cot, slowly cover the decedent's entire body, leaving the head exposed if family members wish to say final farewells
- With each technician at opposite ends of the cot, elevate (raise) the cot to the highest level suitable for loading. Ensure that the legs are locked and secure, then proceed
- If it is determined that the residence's main entrance door can prop itself, exit the residence and load the decedent into the removal vehicle. If not, identify an emotionally stable family member to assist in propping the door for a smooth and efficient exit from the residence

6. Document and Communicate

- ☐ Decedent has no clothes. No accessories. (document and communicate with the appropriate party)
- ☐ Decedent has no personal items being transported to the funeral home (document and communicate with the appropriate party)
- ☐ Decedent appears to be in decent shape and is viewable depending on what disposition the family options (document and communicate with the appropriate party)
- ☐ Decedent has signs of rigor mortis (document and communicate with the appropriate party)
- ☐ Decedent has no paramedic attendance
- ☐ Complete necessary documentation with family (decedent release form, embalming authorization (if applicable), personal effects documentation, etc.)

7. Review and Reflect

- ☐ **Improvement:** Before starting the removal, take a moment to focus and consider all equipment that could be used to increase removal efficiency and effectiveness
- ☐ **Improvement:** Utilize space rather than attempting to work within a confined area that could create claustrophobia or even create a hazardous situation
- ☐ **Improvement:** If the sheet or blanket used to cover the deceased is not soiled and if it is permitted by the family to wrap their loved one in the sheet, then use it. Rather than wasting sheets from our stock that could be used for future removals that require sheet usage
- ☐ **Challenges:** The space in the room was extremely tight but we managed to use the space between the bed and the wall opposite of the deceased to position and prepare the deceased for removal.
- ☐ **Challenges:** The stairs leading up to the main floor were concerning. However, we addressed this challenge by measuring our physical strength by doing a lift test after wrapping the deceased to determine comfort levels. i.e., who would lift the trunk area of the body and the lower extremities
- ☐ **Challenges:** Going up the flight of stairs was challenging. However, we supported each other through constant communication and closeness for leverage of the decedent.
- ☐ **Overall experience:** Perhaps, we could use the Scissor Scoop stretcher with buckles which would be more supporting than carrying with our hands to mitigate the risk of dropping the deceased and straining our backs and other limbs as we carry them to the mortuary cot. This also reduces the time spent on future removals
- ☐ **Overall experience:** Find an open space near the deceased if there is one and prepare the deceased in the space. Please ensure that the family remains upstairs and prepare the deceased in the open area leading into the bedroom. This helps to create more work space. Utilize police and other officials if they are willing to assist. Doing so increases the efficiency of the removal process

8. FollowUp

- ☐ This process will vary considering the distinct protocol and policy to the representing agency, company, or funeral home firm. Complete this step at your own leisure and discretion

SAMPLE | RESIDENTIAL SCENARIO #2

❖ **Location:** Downstairs in the residence

❖ **Decedent's Weight:** 225 lbs.

❖ **Placement:** The decedent is in the bathroom, lying on their side in a tight space between the toilet and bathtub.

❖ **Duration:** Decedent has been in this position for one (1) hour

❖ **Clothing/Accessories:** The decedent is partially clothed, e.g., gym shorts

❖ **Paramedic Attendance:** The decedent was not tended to by paramedics

❖ **Gender:** Male

❖ **Special Note:** The decedent's son wishes to see his loved one once he is positioned on the stretcher, before he is covered.

  ◇ There is a small bruise on the side of the decedent's face due to the fall impact.

1. Assess the Situation
⌸ The residence entrance door (does it prop itself?)
⌸ The decedent is lying on their side between the toilet and bathtub
⌸ The space between the toilet and the bathtub is extremely tight without much wiggle room
⌸ Gym shorts with no shirt
⌸ No paramedic attendance
⌸ No signs of rigor mortis
⌸ No mouth or ear leakage or other body fluid
⌸ Bruise on the cheek of the decedent's face
2. Evaluate Safety Precautions
⌸ Apply PPE, e.g., gloves and facemask, if necessary

3. Plan the Approach

- Consider the space or area where the mortuary cot can be positioned. If there is a hallway leading into the bathroom, position the stretcher two feet from the bathroom door, leaving ample space to work with the decedent
- Prepare the mortuary stretcher before conducting the removal (unbuckle the straps, drape in a linen disposable sheet, place the body cover to the side, and collapse the cot to the floor)
- Only use assistant, no family
- Determine who will lift the trunk and the lower extremities
- Remove the decedent from the bathroom and position on the stretcher
- Determine whether or not the family should exit the home or stay in a designated room until the removal completed

4. Identification

- Before applying the identification, verify the correct spelling of the name with the Next of Kin (NOK) in charge
- Apply the identification bearing the specified information

5. Execute the Removal

- If it is determined that the removal should be private or with limited visibility, kindly instruct all family members to assemble in the front living room area. Inform the family that they can see their loved one after they are prepared and positioned on the stretcher if they so desire
- If there is space in front of the sink, stretch out a white linen sheet. If not, simply proceed to move the decedent from the tight space into the area leading into the bathroom to perform the removal. Proceed with the same removal steps below:
- Tech one: Position oneself over the decedent on the opposite side of the toilet or at the decedent's waste, near the decedent's hand. Tech two: Apply leverage to both legs near the ankles.
- Tech one should leverage the decedent's wrist and lift up a little while tech two pulls. This should release the decedent from this disposition in a liftandpull fashion
- Position the deceased in the middle of the sheet, lying flat on the back, with the legs extended towards the bathroom exit
- This should leave two corners of the sheet in each technician's hands
- Each technician should tie a knot at the head and ankles of the deceased. The deceased should be positioned in the middle of the sheet in a tacolike fashion, wrapped in the sheet, with no body parts exposed
- Make sure no one is visible before proceeding with the removal
- Before execution, one technician should doublecheck the cot to ensure that the legs are locked so as to avoid a collapse when the decedent is placed on the cot
- Both technicians: Bend the knees and leverage the linen sheet, roll up the linen sheet, and lift. Slowly remove the deceased from the floor, carry them out of the bathroom, and position them on the stretcher, ensuring that no skin is exposed
- Fasten each buckle and tighten with care. Finally, with one technician positioned at each end of the cot, slowly cover the decedent's entire body, leaving the head exposed. Next, roll the deceased into an open area (preferably the living room area) for all family members to view their loved one to give final farewells
- With each technician at opposite ends of the cot, elevate (raise) the cot to the highest level suitable for loading. Ensure that the legs are locked and secure, then proceed.
- If it is determined that the residence's main entrance door can prop itself, exit the residence, and load the decedent into the removal vehicle. If not, identify an emotionally stable family member to assist in propping the door for a smooth and efficient exit from the residence

6. Document and Communicate

- ⬦ Decedent is partially clothed with gym shorts. No Accessories (document and communicate with the appropriate party)
- ⬦ Decedent only has on gym shorts and no other personal items being transported to the funeral home (document and communicate with the appropriate party)
- ⬦ Decedent appears to be in decent shape and is viewable depending on what disposition the family options (document and communicate with the appropriate party)
- ⬦ Decedent has no signs of rigor mortis (document and communicate with the appropriate party)
- ⬦ Decedent has no paramedic attendance
- ⬦ Bruise from the impact of the fall on the decedent's face
- ⬦ Complete necessary documentation with family (decedent release form, embalming authorization (if applicable), personal effects documentation, etc.)

7. Review and Reflect

- ⬦ **Improvement:** First, lift and remove the decedent from the space and then move the decedent to an area with sufficient space to prepare the decedent for removal
- ⬦ **Improvement:** As long as the door is concealing and the removal is not visible to family members, the best approach is to tackle the removal in a comfortable and fitting way. For example, putting on shoe covers to stand in the bathtub would have helped leverage a better lift to move the decedent from the constraint
- ⬦ **Challenges:** It was challenging to remove the decedent from the space between the toilet and the bathtub. However, we were able to apply leverage and physical strength to execute the removal. We discussed and determined a strategy and then executed
- ⬦ **Overall Experience:** Utilize spin board to lift the deceased on the mortuary cot. Put the board in the open area leading into the bathroom and carry the decedent to the spin board, lift and position the decedent on the cot. Using the equipment protects and preserves your physicality

8. FollowUp

- ⬦ This process will vary considering the distinct protocol and policy to the representing agency, company, or funeral home firm. Complete this step at your own leisure and discretion

SAMPLE | INSTITUTIONAL SCENARIO #3

❖ **Location:** Emergency Room (ER) at the hospital

❖ **Decedent's Weight:** 165 lbs.

❖ **Presence of Family:** Family is present

❖ **Clothing/Accessories:** The decedent is wearing a patient gown

❖ **Medical Equipment:** Tubing and an IV are attached to the decedent

❖ **Body Bag:** The decedent is not in a body bag

❖ **Special Notes:** The decedent is in a contracted fetal position, with multiple open bed sores, and exhibits purge fluid from the oral and nasal passages. In addition, the decedent does not have hospital/institution identification on ankle or wrist.

◇ The hospital bed is awkwardly positioned and conflicts with the cot

1. Assess the Situation
¤ The decedent is lying in the bed contracted with bed sores
¤ The decedent is not in a body bag
¤ Purging (oral and nasal passages)
¤ Tubing and an IV are attached
¤ Decedent has on a patient gown
¤ Decedent does not have on identification
2. Evaluate Safety Precautions
¤ Utilize a body bag to reduce potential and possible exposure and contamination
¤ Apply PPE, e.g., gloves and facemask, if necessary
¤ Notify a medical professional to remove the tubing and IV only if you lack the confidence to remove them

3. Plan the Approach

- ☐ Place the decedent in a body bag
- ☐ Elevate the bed using the bed controls to be evenly leveled with the mortuary cot
- ☐ Ensure that guard rails are lowered using the bed controls and handles
- ☐ Prepare the mortuary cot before conducting the removaltransfer (unbuckle the straps, drape in a linen disposable sheet, place the body cover to the side, and position the cot near the side of the hospital bed or in an easily accessible area of the room)
- ☐ Only use assistant, no family
- ☐ Determine who will leverage the trunk and the lower extremities
- ☐ Transfer the decedent from the hospital bed and position on the cot
- ☐ Determine whether or not the family should exit the room or wait outside the room until the removal/transfer is complete

4. Identification

- ☐ Before applying the identification, verify the correct spelling of the name with the hospital personnel or next of kin (NOK) in charge
- ☐ Apply the identification bearing the specified information
- ☐ Notify medical professional of the missing identification band and be sure that they apply it to the decedent's person

5. Document and Communicate

- ☐ Decedent is wearing a patient gown. No Accessories (document and communicate with the appropriate party)
- ☐ Decedent does not have any personal items being transported to the funeral home (document and communicate with the appropriate party)
- ☐ Decedent appears to be contracted (document and communicate with the appropriate party)
- ☐ Decedent has no signs of rigor mortis (document and communicate with the appropriate party)
- ☐ Medical Professional (nurse) removed tubing and IV
- ☐ Multiple bed sores, excessive purge fluid from oral and nasal passages
- ☐ Decedent was not in a body bag
- ☐ Family was present
- ☐ Complete necessary documentation with family (decedent release form, embalming authorization, if applicable, personal effects documentation, etc.)

6. Execute the Removal

- Kindly instruct all family members to exit the hospital room. If family members insist on staying, allow them. But inform them that they must remain civilized during the removal process

- If the medical professionals have not removed the tubing and IV, allow them to remove

- If the room has track curtains that hang from the ceiling, close the curtains to reduce visibility and public exposure

- Adjust the hospital bed so you will be able to position the cot beside the bed when you are ready to transfer from the bed to the cot

- **First Method:** The rolltuck, rollpull method should be applied. Before positioning the cot beside the hospital bed, one technician must be positioned on one side of the bed. If assistance is present (removal personnel or medical professional), they should be on the opposite side of the hospital bed. Tech one: roll the patient near the side of the trunk and lower extremities towards their body, allowing technician two to tuck the (unzipped) body bag completely under the decedent's entire body, leaving the top half of the body bag unzipped. Afterward, the technicians should remain in position but switch roles. One technician should now roll the deceased towards them while the other technician pulls the body bag, leaving an even amount of the bag on both sides of the deceased. Each technician should remain as they are, one on each side of the bed. One gently pushes the decedent as the other rolls up the excess body bag and pullposition the decedent on the cot. Before removaltransfer execution, one technician should position the cot beside the bed and doublecheck the cot to ensure that the legs are locked so as to avoid a collapse when the decedent is placed on the cot. **Second Method:** Unzip the entire body bag, leaving only the bottom half of the body bag covering the mortuary cot. Allow the top half that will cover the decedent's face to hang towards the floor. Position the mortuary cot as close as possible, without leaving space between the cot and the bed, on either side of the hospital bed, preferably the side that is easily accessible or closest to the room's exit. The technician should position himself on the side of the cot, using the waste to leverage the pull and transfer of the deceased onto the stretcher, roll up the excess body bag, and pull until the decedent's entire body is positioned on the cot. In case the roll and pull method does not suffice, the tech should grip the mid area or waste line of the decedent and apply a forced pull to execute the transfer. Gentleness is essential, as family sensitivity is important

- Zip the body bag, leaving the decedent's face exposed/visible, and, if possible, instruct the medical professional to apply a name identification sticker or stringed tag with an identification tag to the zipper of the body bag

- Fasten each buckle and tighten with care. Finally, slowly cover the decedent's entire body, leaving the head exposed if family members wish to say final farewells.

- Invite the family back into the room to give farewells

- After the family says farewells, zip the entire body bag and cover and drape the body cover over the body bag, leaving no exposure of the decedent or the body bag from underneath the cover

- Per institution transfer instruction, protocol, or policy, transfer the decedent from the hospital to the removal vehicle

7. Review and Reflect

- **Improvement:** First, instead of using a body bag, save it for another removal and use a patient transfer sheet if there's one underneath the decedent or use one that you have in your removal supply bag. Also, use a linen sheet and tie a knot at the head and the feet of the decedent. For the purge fluid: use a type of absorbent cloth for absorption

- **Challenges:** The main challenge here was attempting to fasten the buckles to secure the deceased considering the body contraction. I had to move one of the straps closest to the strap near the decedent's upper half for more support and security.

- **Overall Experience:** To save time, money on supplies, effort, and energy, identify and employ the easiest and most costefficient method first. The body bag should be utilized for extreme situations, unless they provide one and insist that the decedent is concealed in a body bag due to hospital policy

8. FollowUp

- This process will vary considering the distinct protocol and policy to the representing agency, company, or funeral home firm. Complete this step at your own leisure and discretion

SECTION 1

RESIDENTIAL REMOVALS

LESSONS 4 - 17

Your Favorite Undertaker

The purpose of this exercise is to stimulate critical thinking and problem-solving skills, helping you become a more effective deathcare professional. It also aims to strengthen your interpersonal and verbal communication skills with family members and build the confidence necessary for fieldwork.

Using the 8-step methodology, please solve each scenario. Write your response to how you would solve each removal scenario in the spaces below.

RESIDENTIAL SCENARIO #4

❖ **Location:** Apartment residence, exterior staircase that leads into the entrance

❖ **Decedent's Weight:** 300 lbs.

❖ **Placement:** The decedent is in a cluttered living room area, lying on their back on the floor

❖ **Duration:** Decedent has been in this position for one (1) hour

❖ **Clothing/Accessories:** The decedent is unclothed and covered with a white linen sheet. The decedent has on a wedding band

❖ **Paramedic Attendance:** The decedent was tended to by paramedics

❖ **Gender:** Female

❖ **Special Notes:** The decedent is a hoarder, surrounded by heaps of items. The family wishes to keep the wedding band, but it is difficult to remove due to minor swelling on the decedent's finger. They want to keep it as a keepsake.

　◇ You have to complete a decedent information and release form that requires the decedent's date of birth and time of death, which the family cannot remember

　◇ The amount of junk is so overwhelming that the cot cannot enter the residence. The porch leading into the residence is free of clutter.

1. Assess the Situation

2. Evaluate Safety Precautions

3. Plan the Approach

4. Identification

5. Execute the Removal

6. Document and Communicate

7. Review and Reflect

8. Follow-Up

RESIDENTIAL SCENARIO #5

- ❖ **Location:** Downstairs in the residence

- ❖ **Decedent's Weight:** 150 lbs.

- ❖ **Placement:** The decedent is in the bedroom, in a recliner chair located beside the bed

- ❖ **Duration:** Decedent has been in this position for several hours

- ❖ **Clothing/Accessories:** The decedent has on sleeping wear, and dentures are protruding from the mouth

- ❖ **Paramedic Attendance:** The decedent was not tended to by paramedics

- ❖ **Gender:** Male

- ❖ **Special Notes:** The family is extremely emotional, and some members appear to be under the influence of alcohol. This could potentially hinder the removal process. The police are present at the residence to assist

    - ◇ The room is extremely tight, and the cot cannot fit into the room

1. Assess the Situation

2. Evaluate Safety Precautions

3. Plan the Approach

4. Identification

5. Execute the Removal

6. Document and Communicate

7. Review and Reflect

8. Follow-Up

RESIDENTIAL SCENARIO #6

❖ **Location:** Downstairs in the residence

❖ **Decedent's Weight:** 250 lbs.

❖ **Placement:** The decedent is in the kitchen on the floor, leaning against the cabinets on their side

❖ **Duration:** Decedent has been in this position for one (1) hour

❖ **Clothing/Accessories:** The decedent is partially clothed, e.g., pants, a belt, a gold necklace, and a diamond earring in each ear

❖ **Paramedic Attendance:** The decedent was not tended to by paramedics

❖ **Gender:** Male

❖ **Special Notes:** The family is inside the residence but has expressed that they do not want to witness the removal process or see their loved one covered on the stretcher. This situation is extremely triggering for them, causing fear and discomfort

  ❖ The deceased has $200 in their pants pocket and a cell phone in his pocket that is ringing.

1. Assess the Situation

2. Evaluate Safety Precautions

3. Plan the Approach

4. Identification

5. Execute the Removal

6. Document and Communicate

7. Review and Reflect

8. Follow-Up

RESIDENTIAL SCENARIO #7

- ❖ **Location:** Outside of the residence

- ❖ **Decedent's Weight:** 185 lbs.

- ❖ **Placement:** The decedent is in the front yard, lying on their back on the ground, in front of the residence entrance.

- ❖ **Duration:** Decedent has been in this position for two and a half (2 ½) hours

- ❖ **Clothing/Accessories:** The decedent is fully clothed, e.g., athletic jogging suit, sneakers, right and left ear ring, and pocket book

- ❖ **Paramedic Attendance:** The decedent was tended to by paramedics

- ❖ **Gender:** Female

- ❖ **Special Notes:** Neighbors and family members are visibly present and emotionally distraught. A white linen sheet is draped over the decedent. Police are also present to assist if necessary

  - ◇ The decedent's body seems to be distorted due to the impact of the heart attack

  - ◇ It is very windy outside, the sky looks gloomy, and the forecast predicts a rain storm

1. Assess the Situation

2. Evaluate Safety Precautions

3. Plan the Approach

4. Identification

5. Execute the Removal

6. Document and Communicate

7. Review and Reflect

8. Follow-Up

RESIDENTIAL SCENARIO #8

* **Location:** Residence with exterior entrance stairs and no electricity
* **Decedent's Weight:** 200 lbs.
* **Placement:** The decedent is in the living room area, lying on their back on the couch and wearing soiled clothing. The space is confined.
* **Duration:** Decedent has been in this position for three (3) days
* **Clothing/Accessories:** The decedent is partially clothed, e.g., black tee shirt, socks, and silver bracelet
* **Paramedic Attendance:** The decedent was not tended by paramedics
* **Gender:** Male
* **Special Notes:** The county medical examiner has relinquished jurisdiction because the mother stated that her son had previous medical conditions, allowing the funeral home to perform the removal. Upon arrival, technicians noticed a pipe and a crystal-like substance lying beside the decedent

    ◇ The mother of the decedent is present, but due to her age, she has difficulty walking. She is waiting outside in her vehicle
    ◇ The police are also present
    ◇ Decomposition has set in. Wreaking odor

1. Assess the Situation

2. Evaluate Safety Precautions

3. Plan the Approach

4. Identification

5. Execute the Removal

6. Document and Communicate

7. Review and Reflect

8. Follow-Up

RESIDENTIAL SCENARIO #9

❖ **Location:** Residence in the basement

❖ **Decedent's Weight:** 170 lbs.

❖ **Placement:** The decedent is in the bedroom in the basement area, sitting on the floor in an upright position with their back leaning against the bed

❖ **Duration:** The decedent has been in this position for four (4) hours

❖ **Clothing/Accessories:** The decedent is unclothed, covered with a white linen sheet

❖ **Paramedic Attendance:** The decedent was not tended to by paramedics

❖ **Gender:** Female

❖ **Special Notes:** Several family members are standing in the area, and it is very crowded and compact

  ◇ Upon entrance to the residence, there is a staircase leading into the basement. The space in the basement is limited

1. Assess the Situation

2. Evaluate Safety Precautions

3. Plan the Approach

4. Identification

5. Execute the Removal

6. Document and Communicate

7. Review and Reflect

8. Follow-Up

RESIDENTIAL SCENARIO #10

- ❖ **Location:** Downstairs in the residence
- ❖ **Decedent's Weight:** 125 lbs.
- ❖ **Placement:** The decedent is in the kitchen area, sitting at the dining table
- ❖ **Duration:** The decedent has been in this position for one (1) hour
- ❖ **Clothing/Accessories:** The decedent is fully clothed, e.g., long sleeve button down, pants, socks, loafers, and a timepiece (left wrist)
- ❖ **Paramedic Attendance:** The decedent was not tended by paramedics
- ❖ **Gender:** Male
- ❖ **Special Notes:** The decedent has excessive leakage from the mouth and nose. Despite removal technicians advising her to step into another room as she may not want to remember her loved one this way, the wife refuses to leave the area during the removal process
  - ◇ The wife has one son who has contacted several funeral home providers and never called back to cancel the calls. They both arrive as you were preparing the deceased

1. Assess the Situation

2. Evaluate Safety Precautions

3. Plan the Approach

4. Identification

5. Execute the Removal

6. Document and Communicate

7. Review and Reflect

8. Follow-Up

RESIDENTIAL SCENARIO #11

❖ **Location:** Upstairs in the residence

❖ **Decedent's Weight:** 115 lbs.

❖ **Placement:** The decedent is in a spacious bedroom, lying on their back in the bed, facing up. A blanket is covering the deceased.

❖ **Duration:** The decedent has been in this position for three (3) hours

❖ **Clothing / Accessories:** The decedent is clothed in sleeping wear

❖ **Paramedic Attendance:** The decedent was tended by paramedics

❖ **Gender:** Male

❖ **Special Notes:** The decedent has a wedge pillow under his back. The family's minister is present, and they wish to uphold their tradition of offering prayers over the remains before the deceased is removed from the residence

  ◇ The area upstairs right before entering the bedroom is congested with furniture and other personal items. There is only space for removal personnel to prepare the decedent in the bedroom and carry him out of the bedroom

1. Assess the Situation

2. Evaluate Safety Precautions

3. Plan the Approach

4. Identification

5. Execute the Removal

6. Document and Communicate

7. Review and Reflect

8. Follow-Up

RESIDENTIAL SCENARIO #12

- ❖ **Location:** Downstairs in the residence
- ❖ **Decedent's Weight:** 165 lbs.
- ❖ **Placement:** The decedent is in the bedroom, lying face down on the floor in a narrow space between the dresser and the bed
- ❖ **Duration:** The decedent has been in this position for one (1) day
- ❖ **Clothing/Accessories:** The decedent is clothed in a sleeping gown
- ❖ **Paramedic Attendance:** The decedent was tended by paramedics
- ❖ **Gender:** Female
- ❖ **Special Notes:** The residence is extremely warm due to the central heat. The decedent's clothing items are scattered on the floor, leading into the bedroom. There are even kittens on the bed. The family is present

  - ◇ The residence has black mold on the walls and a mildew odor throughout
  - ◇ The decedent still has a resuscitation kit on his chest from the paramedic attendance

1. Assess the Situation

2. Evaluate Safety Precautions

3. Plan the Approach

4. Identification

5. Execute the Removal

6. Document and Communicate

7. Review and Reflect

8. Follow-Up

RESIDENTIAL SCENARIO #13

❖ **Location:** Downstairs in the residence

❖ **Decedent's Weight:** 400 lbs.

❖ **Placement:** The decedent is in the bathroom lying face down in the bathtub

❖ **Duration:** The decedent has been in this position for two (2) hours

❖ **Clothing / Accessories:** The decedent is unclothed

❖ **Paramedic Attendance:** The decedent was not tended to by paramedics

❖ **Gender:** Female

❖ **Special Notes:** Water is still in the bathtub. The family is gathered in the living area. A family friend who is a firefighter is also present and is willing to help if needed

   ◈ The bathroom has water covering the floor and flowing out of the bathroom into the hallway

   ◈ The bathroom has expensive decor, e.g., floor vases, bench, and a fancy towel rack on the wall

1. Assess the Situation

2. Evaluate Safety Precautions

3. Plan the Approach

4. Identification

5. Execute the Removal

6. Document and Communicate

7. Review and Reflect

8. Follow-Up

RESIDENTIAL SCENARIO #14

- ❖ **Location:** Downstairs in the residence
- ❖ **Decedent's Weight:** 175 lbs.
- ❖ **Placement:** The decedent is in the bathroom, seated on the toilet.
- ❖ **Duration:** Decedent has been in this position for two (2) days
- ❖ **Clothing/Accessories:** The decedent is unclothed with, undergarments found near the ankles
- ❖ **Paramedic Attendance:** The decedent was not tended to by paramedics
- ❖ **Gender:** Male
- ❖ **Special Notes:** The decedent has an unsettling odor, and there are small insects in the bathroom surrounding the toilet. Family members have been asked by police officers to wait outside until the removal process is complete

  - ✧ There is a very loose floorboard right in front of the bathroom entrance
  - ✧ There is ample space in the hall area leading into the bathroom
  - ✧ Signs of skin slip (decomposition)

1. Assess the Situation

2. Evaluate Safety Precautions

3. Plan the Approach

4. Identification

5. Execute the Removal

6. Document and Communicate

7. Review and Reflect

8. Follow-Up

RESIDENTIAL SCENARIO #15

- ❖ **Location:** Downstairs in the residence
- ❖ **Decedent's Weight:** 200 lbs.
- ❖ **Placement:** The decedent is in the bathroom, lying on their back in a confined space
- ❖ **Duration:** The decedent has been in this position for one (1) hour
- ❖ **Clothing/Accessories:** The decedent is partially clothed, wearing a bath towel around the waist
- ❖ **Paramedic Attendance:** The decedent was tended by paramedics
- ❖ **Gender:** Male
- ❖ **Special Notes:** The decedent has excessive bleeding from an abrasion on the forehead, which was caused by the collapse. There is a large blood spill on the floor

  - ◇ The living area and the hall leading into the bathroom are cluttered with lots of personal items
  - ◇ The door leading into the bathroom is so narrow that the cot will not be able to go beyond the living room area

1. Assess the Situation

2. Evaluate Safety Precautions

3. Plan the Approach

4. Identification

5. Execute the Removal

6. Document and Communicate

7. Review and Reflect

8. Follow-Up

RESIDENTIAL SCENARIO #16

❖ **Location:** Upstairs in the residence

❖ **Decedent's Weight:** 185 lbs.

❖ **Placement:** The decedent is in the bedroom, lying face down on the floor

❖ **Duration:** The decedent has been in this position for two (2) hours

❖ **Clothing/Accessories:** The decedent is fully clothed, e.g., polo, jeans, socks, sneakers, timepiece (left wrist), and a diamond ring (right middle finger)

❖ **Paramedic Attendance:** The decedent was not tended by paramedics

❖ **Gender:** Male

❖ **Special Notes:** The decedent is experiencing excessive leakage from the mouth and is emitting groaning sounds due to gas releases. The family members wish to assist in the removal process of their loved one

   ◇ The decedent is lying on the side of the bed, and his face is face down on a mat that can leave imprints on his face that could distort his face and affect viewing

   ◇ The bedroom is spacious; however, the bed is extremely close to the wall, and the decedent is lying on the side closest to the wall and not on the side that is spacious entering the bedroom.

   ◇ There is an open area outside of the bedroom where the family is assembled

1. Assess the Situation

2. Evaluate Safety Precautions

3. Plan the Approach

4. Identification

5. Execute the Removal

6. Document and Communicate

7. Review and Reflect

8. Follow-Up

RESIDENTIAL SCENARIO #17

❖ **Location:** Downstairs in the residence

❖ **Decedent's Weight:** 195 lbs.

❖ **Placement:** The decedent is in a narrow hallway area, lying face down on the floor

❖ **Duration:** The decedent has been in this position for one (1) week

❖ **Clothing/Accessories:** The decedent is partially clothed, e.g., undergarments

❖ **Paramedic Attendance:** The decedent was not tended by paramedics

❖ **Gender:** Female

❖ **Early Decomposition Phase:** The decedent is near a floor heater and has excessive blood-containing foam leakage from the mouth and nose. Additionally, the stomach is extremely bloated

❖ **Special Notes:** There is feces throughout the home left by the decedent's dog

   ✧ The living area leading into the narrow hall has a couch that is also covered in feces that is slightly blocking the hall entrance

1. Assess the Situation

2. Evaluate Safety Precautions

3. Plan the Approach

4. Identification

5. Execute the Removal

6. Document and Communicate

7. Review and Reflect

8. Follow-Up

SECTION 2

INSTITUTIONAL REMOVALS

LESSONS 18 - 25

Your Favorite Undertaker

8-Step Systematic Methodology

1. Assess the Situation

- Identify the location of the decedent.
- Note any environmental factors (e.g., temperature, lighting, space constraints).
- Determine the condition of the decedent (e.g., clothing, position, signs of decomposition).

2. Evaluate Safety Precautions

- Ensure personal protective equipment (PPE) is worn.
- Assess the need for additional assistance or specialized equipment (e.g., lifting devices, body bags).

3. Plan the Approach

- Determine the best approach for moving the decedent based on the scenario.
- Consider the need for coordination with other professionals or authorities or family members (e.g., medical examiner, law enforcement).

4. Identification

- Apply the correct identification to the decedent's person.

5. Document and Communicate

- Record relevant details of the removal process (e.g., condition of the decedent, any observations).
- Communicate with relevant parties (e.g., family members, funeral director, medical professional, or medical examiner) as necessary.

6. Execute the Removal

- Follow established protocols for handling and moving the decedent.
- Use proper lifting techniques and equipment to avoid injury.
- Maintain dignity and respect for the decedent throughout the process.

7. Review and Reflect

- Evaluate the removal process for areas of improvement.
- Consider any challenges faced and how they were addressed.
- Reflect on the overall experience to enhance future removals.

8. Follow - Up

- Ensure the decedent is properly transported to the designated facility.
- Complete any required documentation or paperwork associated with the removal.
- Provide any necessary support or information to the family or other involved parties.

Using the **8-step methodology**, please solve each scenario. Write your response to how you would solve each removal scenario in the spaces below.

INSTITUTIONAL SCENARIO #18

- ❖ **Location:** Emergency Room (ER) at the hospital
- ❖ **Decedent's Weight:** 200 lbs.
- ❖ **Presence of Family:** Family is not present
- ❖ **Clothing / Accessories:** The decedent is fully clothed
- ❖ **Medical Equipment:** No tubing or IV is attached to the decedent
- ❖ **Body Bag:** The decedent is in a vinyl body bag
- ❖ **Special Notes:** The decedent has medical needles in the bed, a shock device attached to their chest, an oxygen mask, and a patient sheet underneath them.

1. Assess the Situation

2. Evaluate Safety Precautions

3. Plan the Approach

4. Identification

5. Document and Communicate

6. Execute the Removal

7. Review and Reflect

8. Follow-Up

INSTITUTIONAL SCENARIO #19

❖ **Location:** Patient Room (ICU - Fourth (4th) floor)

❖ **Decedent's Weight:** 135 lbs.

❖ **Presence of Family:** Family is present

❖ **Clothing/Accessories:** The decedent is wearing a patient gown

❖ **Medical Equipment:** Tubing and an IV are attached to the decedent

❖ **Body Bag:** The decedent is in a vinyl body bag, covered with a white sheet, with the face still visible

❖ **Special Notes:** The family states they are headed to the funeral home shortly after your departure with their loved one. However, the office is closed, and they insist on meeting with a licensed funeral director to start the arrangement process

1. Assess the Situation

2. Evaluate Safety Precautions

3. Plan the Approach

4. Identification

5. Document and Communicate

6. Execute the Removal

7. Review and Reflect

8. Follow-Up

INSTITUTIONAL SCENARIO #20

- ❖ **Location:** Hospital Morgue/Refrigeration System
- ❖ **Decedent's Weight:** 350 lbs.
- ❖ **Placement:** The decedent is in a two-body, side loading cooler on the bottom shelf
- ❖ **Presence of Family:** Family is not present
- ❖ **Clothing/Accessories:** The decedent is wearing a patient gown
- ❖ **Medical Equipment:** No tubing or IVs are attached to the decedent
- ❖ **Body Bag:** The decedent is in a vinyl body bag
- ❖ **Special Notes:** The body bag is a standard-size body bag, which is too small and has a rip down the side of the seam, and the decedent has fluid leakage

1. Assess the Situation

2. Evaluate Safety Precautions

3. Plan the Approach

4. Identification

5. Document and Communicate

6. Execute the Removal

7. Review and Reflect

8. Follow-Up

INSTITUTIONAL SCENARIO #21

❖ **Location:** Hospital Morgue/Refrigeration System

❖ **Decedent's Weight:** 250 lbs.

❖ **Placement:** The decedent is on a morgue table in a walk-in cooler with ten other decedents. Positioned near the back, the decedent needs to be shifted toward the front for removal from the cooler

❖ **Presence of Family:** Family is not present

❖ **Clothing/Accessories:** The decedent is wearing a patient gown and has personal items attached to be transported with them to the funeral home

❖ **Medical Equipment:** Tubing and an IV are not attached to the decedent

❖ **Body Bag:** The decedent is in a vinyl body bag

❖ **Special Notes:** There is a spacious area outside the walk-in cooler

1. Assess the Situation

2. Evaluate Safety Precautions

3. Plan the Approach

4. Identification

5. Document and Communicate

6. Execute the Removal

7. Review and Reflect

8. Follow-Up

INSTITUTIONAL SCENARIO #22

- ❖ **Location:** County Medical Examiner's Office

- ❖ **Decedent's Weight:** 600 lbs.

- ❖ **Placement:** The decedent is on an oversized morgue table in a walk-in cooler. The forensics agent enters the cooler to remove the decedent

- ❖ **Assistance Aid:** Ceiling lift with a heavy-duty design, capable of lifting up to 1000 lbs.

- ❖ **Presence of Family:** Family is not present

- ❖ **Clothing / Accessories:** The decedent is unclothed due to autopsy

- ❖ **Medical Equipment:** No tubing or IVs are attached to the decedent

- ❖ **Body Bag:** The decedent is in a vinyl body bag

- ❖ **Special Note:** The decedent has personal items to be transported to the funeral home with them. The items that were presented and transferred included personal identification (ID), a social security card, cigarettes, a lighter, and $500. The medical examiner provided an itemized document with the items listed, but several valuable items listed on the list were not included with the items to be transferred.

1. Assess the Situation

2. Evaluate Safety Precautions

3. Plan the Approach

4. Identification

5. Document and Communicate

6. Execute the Removal

7. Review and Reflect

8. Follow-Up

INSTITUTIONAL SCENARIO #23

- ❖ **Location:** Nursing home facility
- ❖ **Decedent's Weight:** 100 lbs.
- ❖ **Placement:** The decedent is lying in a healthcare bed on their back
- ❖ **Presence of Family:** Family is present
- ❖ **Clothing/Accessories:** The decedent is wearing a patient gown
- ❖ **Medical Equipment:** Tubing and an IV are not attached to the decedent
- ❖ **Body Bag:** The decedent is not a vinyl body bag
- ❖ **Special Notes:** Upon your arrival, the nurse stated that the agency/funeral home you represent is not listed on the paperwork to release the decedent. The face sheet that was provided does not have the correct name of the decedent

  - ✧ The decedent is covered up to the neck with a white linen blanket and has a towel under their mouth to keep it closed
  - ✧ The mattress is an inflated air mattress with alternating controls attached to the bed, which is elevated near the head
  - ✧ The decedent is wearing a ring and a necklace. Additionally, they do not share the room with another patient
  - ✧ The decedent has a visible open sore on the left side of their head

1. Assess the Situation

2. Evaluate Safety Precautions

3. Plan the Approach

4. Identification

5. Document and Communicate

6. Execute the Removal

7. Review and Reflect

8. Follow-Up

INSTITUTIONAL SCENARIO #24

❖ **Location:** Nursing home facility

❖ **Decedent's Weight:** 185 lbs.

❖ **Placement:** The decedent is lying in a healthcare bed on their back

❖ **Presence of Family:** Family is not present

❖ **Clothing / Accessories:** The decedent is wearing a patient gown and assistive heel protectors

❖ **Medical Equipment:** Tubing and an IV are not attached to the decedent

❖ **Body Bag:** The decedent is not a vinyl body bag

❖ **Special Notes:** The decedent is covered in a white blanket and shares a room with another patient who is still alive

◇ The room has ceiling track curtains to provide privacy between them

◇ The bed does not have an alternative system but can be adjusted using a bed crank at the end. The bed has been lowered

◇ The decedent has dentures on the nightstand, not concealed in a casing

1. Assess the Situation

2. Evaluate Safety Precautions

3. Plan the Approach

4. Identification

5. Document and Communicate

6. Execute the Removal

7. Review and Reflect

8. Follow-Up

INSTITUTIONAL SCENARIO #25

❖ **Location:** Hospice Care Facility

❖ **Decedent's Weight:** 150 lbs.

❖ **Placement:** The decedent is lying in a healthcare bed on their back

❖ **Presence of Family:** Family is present

❖ **Clothing/Accessories:** The decedent is wearing a patient gown

❖ **Medical Equipment:** Tubing and an IV are not attached to the decedent

❖ **Body Bag:** The decedent is not a vinyl body bag

❖ **Special Notes:** Per the company/firm policy you represent, you need a face sheet or something equivalent but the nurse/staff is unable to provide one due to their printer being down

  ✧ The decedent has a head covering lying on the pillow near their head. The cause of death was a rare cancer

  ✧ The decedent has a colostomy bag attached, which appears to be filled

  ✧ One family member (the son) insists on assisting with the removal as it will provide a sense of closure

  ✧ They also asked when someone should be in touch with them to further expedite the process

1. Assess the Situation

2. Evaluate Safety Precautions

3. Plan the Approach

4. Identification

5. Document and Communicate

6. Execute the Removal

7. Review and Reflect

8. Follow-Up

ABOUT THE AUTHOR

Marco Thomas, owner of Eden Logistics Inc., based in Memphis, TN, has been in the removal service industry for eight years and possesses extensive experience and training in various types of removals. Eden Logistics serves funeral homes, medical examiners, and organ/tissue donor providers throughout the tri-state area and beyond. Thomas has facilitated thousands of removals, both local and distant, and continues to strive to provide the best possible service to the death care industry.

Thomas offers invaluable resources to help death care professionals sharpen their skills and critical thinking and become effective in their roles. Some of these resources include CEUs, public speaking engagements, and workshops.

For more information about these resources and how to partner with us, please see the information below!

Eden Logistics Inc
Contact: (901) 713-2650
Email Address: EdenLogisticsinc@gmail.com

Scan Here!

Your Favorite Undertaker

Ride With After Life aims to educate teenagers about the mortuary industry while helping them make better long-term decisions that affect their quality of life. The program's ultimate goal is to raise awareness among inner-city youth about the consequences of crimes and poor decisions.

Participants will have the opportunity to engage in the mortuary transport process and learn about careers in funeral and post-mortem care through valuable mentorship. They will also gain insight into how decisions made today can impact mortality, including choices related to healthy eating, exercise, and avoiding drug use and violent crime.

The program provides an eye-opening experience for youth, highlighting the consequences of unhealthy behavior. Participants will leave feeling encouraged and empowered to make positive changes in their lives.

For more information on how teenagers can sign up, please refer to the information below.

Scan Here!

Eden Logistics Inc., a premier mortuary removal and transport business, proudly serves Memphis, Tennessee, and the Mid-South region. Specializing in removals from medical facilities, funeral homes, and residences, Eden Logistics Inc. is dedicated to delivering professional and compassionate service. Our highly trained staff and technologically advanced scheduling process aim to alleviate the stress associated with post-mortem care.

Committed to serving licensed funeral professionals and affiliates, Eden Logistics Inc. promises timely removals and transports coupled with competitive pricing and the utmost professionalism. Our mission is to provide superior transport services to mortuaries, funeral homes, medical institutions, certified coroners, and affiliates within the Tri-State area. We uphold this mission through the following services:

⋄ Competitive flat rates for local removals and transfers

⋄ 24/7 availability

⋄ Local and long-distance removal and transport services

⋄ Highly trained staff and clean, fully equipped removal vans

Our service offerings not only save your firm valuable time but also reduce employee wage and removal vehicle costs and maintenance. Our goal is to eliminate the stress associated with the removal and transport process, allowing your business to focus on funeral planning and services.

We welcome the opportunity to meet with your team and discuss how Eden Logistics Inc. can contribute to the success of your company. To schedule a meeting, please contact us at 901-713-2650 or by emailing EdenLogisticsInc@gmail.com.

Made in United States
Orlando, FL
24 August 2024